Praise for *Meister Eckhart's Book of the Heart*

"In the ecstatic spirit of Rumi and Hafiz, Meister Eckhart's words dance and invite the reader into an intimate encounter with the divine. Reading these poems sets the heart ablaze and the spirit soaring."

—Christine Valters Paintner, PhD,
author of *The Artist's Rule:*
Nurturing Your Creative Soul with Monastic Wisdom

"In reading *Meister Eckhart's Little Book of the Heart*, it again came to mind why I am so drawn to the poetry of Rumi, Hafiz, and Kabir. There is revelation in this book by Burrows and Sweeney. I sincerely feel it will help one look deeper into the eyes of the Christ and know more of God's knowledge and love."

—Daniel Ladinsky, international bestselling author of
I Heard God Laughing, A Year with Hafiz,
Love Poems from God, and other books of poetry

"I think Mark Burrows and Jon Sweeney achieve something quite rare and wonderful here. They make Eckhart clear, concise, and very compelling!

—Richard Rohr, OFM, bestselling author of
Falling Upward, Breathing Under Water

"If for many of us a dose of Meister Eckhart is like a morning pot of coffee, this concentrated and poetic reduction is like a book full of double espresso shots—each is about as much as you can take in and metabolize in a day."

—Brother Paul Quenon, Abbey of Gethsemani,
author of *Unquiet Vigil*

"The mystical vision of Eckhart uses words and imagery, not to define the Mystery, but to lead us into it. Likewise, these new renderings delight the mind and penetrate the soul, as Eckhart did centuries ago and continues to do in every age. They are a delight in themselves and a gift to those who travel the wayless way."

—Anthony J. Finnerty, chairman of
The Eckhart Society (UK)

Meister Eckhart's
Book of the Heart

Meditations for the Restless Soul

Jon M. Sweeney and Mark S. Burrows

HAMPTON ROADS

Cover design by Jim Warner
Cover photograph Sunflowers I, (oil on canvas), Bratby, John (1928–92)
Private Collection / Photo © Christie's Images / Bridgeman Images
Interior by Kathryn Sky-Peck
Typeset in Truesdell

Hampton Roads Publishing Company, Inc.
Charlottesville, VA 22906
Distributed by Red Wheel/Weiser, LLC
www.redwheelweiser.com

Sign up for our newsletter and special offers by going to
www.redwheelweiser.com/newsletter/.

ISBN: 978-1-57174-764-8

Library of Congress Cataloging-in-Publication Data
available upon request

Printed in Canada
MAR

10 9 8 7 6 5 4 3 2 1

CONTENTS

THESE ARE POEMS BY MEISTER ECKHART. . .

. . . the 14th century German mystic, philosopher, friar, priest, and theologian. There's only one problem: Eckhart never wrote poems. He wrote in discursive prose: his academic works in Latin and many of his sermons in the German vernacular of his day. But his manner of expression, despite the formalities of genre, is often poetic to the core.

He also wrote at a time when the monastic orders were in turmoil, the papacy had fled to Avignon, apocalyptic fears and prophecies abounded, and his fellow Dominican friars as those charged with administering the Inquisition were hunting heretics all over the countryside. In the midst of all that, Meister Eckhart captured the many forms and stages of the love of God, the mystic path found in the most ordinary of moments, and the journey of transformation—all this in language so startling that he himself came under suspicion as a heretic. This was a time when original thinking and daring theological formulations were suspect. Yet his thought has endured and even flourished, in part because of the authenticity that rings throughout. Seven centuries later, we felt it was time to find the gems in his prose, the essence of his soul-penetrating ideas, and render these in verse.

This book gives voice to the startling wonderings and wonderful wanderings of one who, already in his lifetime, came to be called the *Meister*, or "Master." The poems found here are not a translation, narrowly construed, but rather our attempts at voicing—or re-voicing—his thought. They take the first-person confessional form, with the occasional self-reflective poem written as if by Eckhart to himself. As such, the book enters into the surprising depths of Eckhart's poetic mind in order to offer the insights he formulated in an idiom accessible to late-modern readers. For these are times when many among us find our restlessness of heart and longing for the sacred unsatisfied by the settled and often formal conventions of religious discourse, and long for something other or more. This book is an invitation to the adventure held in this journey we call life.

The result, we hope, will be a whole new discovery of this extraordinary mystic. For he really is the Christian Rumi, the ecstatic Catholic's Kabir, the Dominican Hafiz. He was and is a bard who calls us in and through and beyond our thinking and feeling to what he sensed was the heart of our life: the art of being authentically human.

Opening the Heart's Door

> Ours is not the work
> of seeking You here
> or there where we
>
> think You might be,
> but of opening
> the heart's door,
>
> and when we do this
> You cannot resist
> coming in, since
>
> our opening and Your
> entering are one: You
> knock and wait, and
>
> when we open we
> find that You were
> there all along and
>
> will not leave us.

Part One

OUR SOUL-LIFE

Look Quietly

> What it is that hurts
> baffles
> or befalls me
> might just be
> concealing the God
> whom I love.

Sometimes You Have to Break Things

It's true:
Sometimes you have
to break things
if you want
to grasp God in them.
In the breaking,
we allow what's holy
to take form
in us.

What Do You See?

To you
who knows
God
as God
knows you,
happiness is
heavenly,
and, like all
blessed ones,
you will
see only
One.

Nine Words of Prayer

God, our only,
Scripture, our gift,
Holy, the qualities we seek.

The Name, sweet on the lips,
the Love, intimate and secret,
Humility, again and again.

Vain is the world;
Miserable, those apart;
and Blessed, the sainthood
    we seek.

Can You Do This?

"You have died, and your life is hidden with Christ in God."

—*Colossians 3:3*

The soul that wants nothing but God
  must forsake everything,
  even God.
As long as we have and know who
  God is, we don't.
  We are far away.
So can you let your notions die?
  This is the smallest death a soul can undergo before
  it becomes divine.

Can You See?

> If you want
> to be ready for
> and worthy of
> the Spirit of God,
> just look inside and see
> your spiritual being.
> Can you see
> how you already
> resemble
> what you seek?

What I Want Is Joy

What I want is joy.
What You teach me

is that suffering is
the way, letting go

is the truth, and no-
thingness is the life.

Which is after all
what I need.

Your Silence

> There is a language so
> beautiful that it is never spoken.
> There is a deep sort of silence
> that may never adequately fall into words.
> That, I tell you, is more valuable
> than any jewel
> or any diamond.

Room to Grow

> My life is like a page on which
> so much is already written:
>
> hurts and joys and the tumble
> of fears and uncertainties.
>
> What You want of me, God, is
> that I clean the slate, emptying
>
> it of all this to make room for
> the freedom of nothingness
>
> where alone You, my God,
> have room to grow.

All and Ever Only Love

I often wonder if I am lovable,
and love cautiously because

I know how easily I can be
hurt and my heart broken,

but You do not hesitate
toward me, since You

are all love and only love,
and when You love You

love without measure, and
when You love me in

this way I find who I am
and who You are, which

is all and ever only love.

Obedience

> is a form of love: I taste
> it when I let my will stir
>
> into practice a sense of the
> goodness that my vision
>
> inspires in my heart.

Breaking Through

Too often I decide what my
life should be and whether

there is room in it for You
while You sit in a deeper

place within me, wondering
what it will take for me to

make more of all the things
in my life—the good and

the bad—and so learn to
break through to find You

in all that is and let You
take form in me in all that

I was and am and will be.

A Soul Digests

Each of us has a soul
made to grasp the One
who made every one,
body and soul.
Slowly and deliberately,
as bodies digest, the soul's powers
move and nourish us.
As the body grows, the soul's powers
grow inside us.
As my eyes learn to see,
in light and all detail, the soul
finds its power to think and see.

The Way Love Is

> You are love in everything
> that is, and it belongs to
>
> the perfection of Your greatness
> that not even my nothingness
>
> is far from You, for You
> meet me in my imperfection
>
> and You act on me not from
> the distance of my failings
>
> but from the presence
> of Your perfection which
>
> is the way love is.

A Single Undivided Love

When I open my heart to receive You
in times of peace and quiet, this is as

it should be, but if I close my heart
to You when I have lost my way and

my life is a mess, I have failed to know
the truth, for these differ only for me

but not for You, for Your heart opens
to me with a single undivided love.

In Each Moment

Oh, teach me in each moment
of every Now to know that

You are the Here in all my
wandering and the Yes in

all my wondering and the Love
in nothing less than everything.

The One

There is within me a citadel where I am one with You,
a place so strong and pure that no one—not even You—

dares to look inside, unless You strip Yourself of all
Your names and natures, to the point where You

are one and simple, for only there, beyond all
doing and thinking and feeling, can You know

the one I am and can I know the one You are.

Consider the Moon

Remember the moon as it wanes and fills
among the clouds,
at holy days.
Consider the moon: it is closer
to the earth than any star or planet.
It pales in comparison to these.
Its light does not sparkle.
It's spotted, mottled.
Oceans wax and wane with the moon.
But the morning star,
how different,
is always present.
It is always and equally near,
shining in the sky before the sun
overwhelms us,
raised above earthly concerns
as your soul should be.

Gratitude

We should not thank You
because You love us,
but thank You
that You are so good
that You cannot do anything else!

In All That Is

Most days, I am clear
about what is right

and wrong, good
and bad, in and out,

but when I have
You close to me

in my heart I see
how You shine in

all that is, especially
in my often

darkened life.

Study the Stone

Be yourself. And if what this means
is unclear to you, look around at

the things of this earth. Study the stone
which always does what it was made

to do: it doesn't always fall in the
same way, sometimes resting in high

places and at other times finding its
rest where the earth allows it to lie,

but its purpose is to move downward,
and in this the stone loves God in the

way it can, singing the new song
which God gives each creature and thing—

and also you who read this and at times
wonder what to do and how to be.

You Taste Us

It sounds as strange as it is true
to say, as I have never said before,

that You taste Yourself and in this
taste every creature that You ever

made which crawls or swims or flies,
on earth, in the seas, and upon the

blue-flung skies. And when You
taste Yourself in all these, and even

in me, You taste us all as You ever
are in the oneness of Yourself.

Becoming Love, I

If I wish to
become one
with You

and come
to know You
as You are

I must set
aside my words
and become

a nothingness
spacious enough
for Your all-ness,

and in this
You transform
me wholly

into the
one Love You
ever are.

The Descent of Love

In distress and want I ask, "Where, O God, are You?"
Here, I am as close to you as the warmth of your breath.

But this does not satisfy my mind, and so I ask again.
Here, in the confusions that make you trade life for death.

Still I ask what I have with my questions already said.
Here, in the doubts that rise against My descending truth.

And yet I am undone with deceptions ever old and new.
Here, let me give Myself to you with love that alone will soothe.

Emptiness

If I hope to find You,
I need to let go

of all I think I need
to know, turning

from what I desire
to become the

emptiness You
cannot resist.

Outside of Space and Time

Outside of
space and time
there is no work,
nothing is wrought.
Time stops.

Be there
and don't look away
because in that place
your soul and God
are one.

Love's Delights

I sometimes think You are the reverse
of gravity, causing everything to rise,
from the heavy earth up to the highest skies,

but you show me that Yours is the work of
coming down, of weighting what is light

so that I, like You, might enter into what
is least and raise it up to sound love's
delight in heaven's proper height.

If I Hope to Know You

I must seek an unknowing
that is not a lack but

my only gain, taking me
beyond the press

of demands and desires
to an emptiness

where there is room for
You to be born

beyond all that I demand
to know and desire

to find, for You birth
Your Word in the space

of my silence and burn
as light in my dark.

An Unknowing That Makes Room

> I often think it is my work
> to find You, and in the
>
> tangle of my life I stumble
> into brambles of doubt
>
> and pits of uncertainties
> and wonder where You
>
> are hiding, and then I
> remember: You seek
>
> and I am found.

Joy Meets Joy

In my hurry, I often
forget that You desire

to seek those who
have gone astray,

even me, and that
my work is to free

myself of myself
so that You can be

born in me, and so
your joy in seeking

meets my joy in
having been found.

You Rise by Stooping Down

With You everything
is upside down

and inside out,
for You rise by

stooping down,
and call me

to follow in
the footsteps

of your descent,
where I find

that You and
I are one

in being and
even in power.

A Human Heart Pounds

A human
heart
pounds
to live
and to
give
life.

But that
same
heart
is a
mystical
place
that can
love
the
Lord God
with
each
quiet
beat.

How We Fit

You made us for Yourself,
and we fit not as one part

to another but rather as
emptiness meets fullness,

as darkness seeks light,
as loneliness wants love,

as what is wounded
longs for healing.

Nothing of My Deeds

When I am in the wrong mind
I presume that You desire
    my goodness,
but when my mind turns aright
I find that You want nothing
    of my deeds
and everything of my heart.

God's Unending Now

To say as many do that God made the world
is to confuse what is true, for God never ceased

making what was made, and what will be
is already present in God's unending Now.

This truth reminds me that God is making
all things new, even what is past and gone

and also what lies yet unknown in the future—
in your life and mine.

Risking Unknowing

How should I prepare to find You?
In emptying myself of the chatter

of my words, and opening myself
to the silence that allows me

to risk an unknowing that expects
nothing and deserves nothing

and wills nothing other than
the word You speak in

the stillness I keep where
my wandering ceases and

my wondering begins?

More God

I want more love.
Which is to say,

more God.

I want more God
in everything.

More love.

In everything.

In and through and
beyond it all.

More God.

Part Two

LETTING GO

The Rest

Don't try to find God.
Simplify your scattered life,
and become one
in yourself.
Then God will
find you. The rest
will follow.

Our Secret Entry

What is our secret entry
into Your heart?

We find it on the path of
letting go of what we

thought we knew, arriving
at the place where we

know nothing of knowing
beyond every notion of love,

and from light enter
the dark only to find

ourselves there, ever
one with You.

Alternatives

There is only ever one path
you are on when you are on the
path to God.
Many ways may suggest themselves;
many good alternatives may come.
Just gather them to that
one path that
is already yours
that is God's
that is yours.

The Man with Money

There was once a man who
had a hundred dollars.
He lost forty, but still, he had sixty.
I tried to comfort him,
saying, "You have sixty bucks,
my friend!"
But all he could do was
gaze upon his suffering.
Lovers, they would sit and stare
into each other's eyes,
clinging.

This Is What You Desired

Now listen, Eckhart, to Seneca,
such wisdom from the pagan philosopher!
What is it that will console you when
you are troubled or suffering?
This is simple:
accept that what you have
is exactly what you desired,
what you prayed for.
Or you would have desired it,
had you known
    the will of God.

Don't Work So Hard

At the heart of things is an eternal present
moment which is in each and every thing

that is—and in me and in you, and when
we let ourselves come into an awareness of

this Now we come to know ourselves as
a becoming-new without renewal, and this

is the truth beyond all our worries and needs
and hopes, this one eternal present moment.

Lose Yourself!

Make a start with yourself
by abandoning yourself.

For if you do not begin
by taking leave of who

you are, everything
you do or think you are

and all you seek will be
an obstacle for you, and

you will be like one
who has lost her way

and in wandering only
becomes further lost,

so if you wish to find
your way, lose yourself!

Becoming Love, II

When I learn to love You
simply because You are love,

I come to accept myself simply
because You made me in love

and You never stop making me.
And when I hold onto this and

let go of every doubt, I find
Your love in everything

and I become love in You
and You become love in me.

Where I Stop, You Begin

Often I think I
should find You
within myself,
but it isn't so:
only when I let
go of myself
with all my
wants and needs,
for the sake of
Your love, do I
find You, for
in Your love You
go completely
outside Yourself

to find me.

Letting Go

I don't like the dark.
I'd rather be clothed
than naked.

Yet You tell me
I must let go of all that
clothes me—

my joys and fears,
my worries and even
my imaginings—

and give myself
to the dark emptiness
where You wait

to be born in me.

Enough

If I could learn to let go of what I
have and was and will be, of all

the good gifts You have given,
then I could trust myself to

know who I truly *am*, which
is the only one You desire,

for You are ever love, and I
am ever loved, and it is enough

to know and be Your beloved.

Truth Does Not Like Business Deals

When I seek what You alone
can give, what I find is my seeking,

like the wager of a business deal
in which I hope for payment for

my efforts, but You who are always
already within me do not seek me,

and so You do not desire my finding
but seek rather the emptiness by which

I might unclutter my life of all that
I am, even my faith, even my desire

to seek You, for this You cannot resist.

What Then of You?

We think of things as this or that,
as better or worse, as good or bad,

but in God everything is what it
is and lives in the perfection of

its being, which is to say that the
little fly as it exists in God is

nobler than the highest angel
is in itself. What then of me?

What then of you?

Making Space

What You are able to do
in me depends on the quality

of my life and whether there
is enough space for You to

act as You wish to do, and
my work is simply to shake

myself loose of what I
think or expect You desire

so that You might find
in my naked nothingness

enough room for You to
be the love You ever are

and long to set free in me.

Become Empty

> So you want to find God?
> Empty yourself of everything—
>
> your worries and your hopes,
> your wishes and your fears.
>
> For when you are finally
> empty, God will find you,
>
> because God cannot tolerate
> emptiness and will come
>
> to fill you with himself.

We Must Abandon God

One person said they had God,
while another lamented God's absence.

I say this: we must abandon the God
we have in our thinking and believing

for God's sake, so that we might come
to know God as God truly is—who

never left us, beyond knowing, in
a single oneness and pure union.

Only My Nothingness

When I learn to let go of who I think I am
and relinquish all I think I need to be me,

You cannot resist entering my heart, and do,
for when I let go of thinking that my life is mine

You finally have room to make it Yours and
cannot help but come to fill what is empty,

for You want only my nothingness and to
that You give Your allness, and so I shall know

Your heart as mine and mine as Yours.

Desiring Nothing and Seeking Nothing

> If we could rest in the one truth
> that You are, beyond our need
>
> to understand and on the far side
> of our fear of failing, we could
>
> learn to live without desiring
> something else than who we are,
>
> and then we could begin to love
> without needing to know why.

A Single Mind

The strongest prayer I could ever pray
and the one that will give me no less

than everything is the one that proceeds
from a single mind, simple and uncluttered

of my *I*, for in this emptying, when I want
nothing more for myself, You cannot help

but come and give me all You will and all
You are of Yourself, and in the meeting

of this gift You become who You truly are
and I become who I truly am and come

to know that in this we are one single One.

Even More

We should
know that no
one in this life
has learned
to let go who
could not
learn
to let go
even more.

Forgetting to Remember

Too often I forget who I am,
and begin to listen to what

they say about me, and so
forget what is my one and

only work: to remember
that I am the one You love,

which is all I have ever
been and all I need to be.

Paradox

The more I want of me
the less I have of You,

and the more I want
of You the less I have

of me, because if I
could ever have enough

of You to be content,
what I would have

would not be You but
only my desire for You.

Only when I let go

of what others say,
and listen to who

I truly am, do I make
room for the one me

You want me to be.

Love Is the Lure

> When the fish takes the hook,
> the fisherman has it no matter
>
> how it twists and turns. So
> it is with love: when we take
>
> hold of it, it holds us like a
> hook, and nothing can take it
>
> from us or us from You.

Moses

On that holy mountain
the lonely man dared
not look, and
hid his face.

On that windy outcrop
the single man was deathly
afraid even to lift his eyes
above the rocks.

Only when he, lonely and alone,
turned away from what he knew
were the hidden things of God
suddenly before him.

Behind You

There is a wanting of God
so much
that you are willing
to forsake everything
godly to find him.
Ponder this,
the God who is beyond
what is godly.
Know this,
that you may have to leave
more than you ever imagined
behind.

Sweet Darkness

There is
a reason
why we
call it
supernatural
when we
meet grace
so holy and
the breath of life
lonely in the
darkness
above.

Jesus in the Temple

There is no need to wonder why
Jesus threw everyone out of the temple
that day.
He wanted it empty.
The temple is inside of you and
the Lord wants it all to himself.

Good People

You may fast and pray and
do good works. Oh yes, you should!
But if you ever imagine that all those
things you do are some transaction,
oh no.
God is not in business.
God only wants a temple that is
perfectly and completely
empty.

Every Angel

A theologian once taught that the angels around us here on earth are unhappy compared with those that surround God in heaven. Nonsense!

Every angel does the will of the One who sent it and God's work is good equally and everywhere.

Were the Holy One to have an angel in the trees for picking off caterpillars, that would be the greatest joy imaginable.

What then should I do

>
> but dare to let go of my wish to be
> something or someone, and let You
>
> be nothing and no one, and so let
> my being-me sink into Your
>
> being-You and so my me and
> Your You become one single One.

Unlearning

—to the memory of Elizabeth Bishop

Lesson I

> *What is the purpose of creation?*
> That every thing might simply be.
> *Why does God give, and then take away?*
> God doesn't. God gives that
> every thing might be.
> *Why create at all, God?*
> Why?
>   Because, that is what I do.

Lesson II

Is every creation from God?
Every single one.
*How does one know that creation has
taken place?*
Every creation breathes.
What else?
There is love.
And . . . ?
There is rest.
Yes . . .
Satisfaction, joy, and delight.

Lesson III

Which created thing is better than the others?
You misunderstand.
Which one shines brighter?
You are not listening.
What is the purpose of each?
Be quiet.
Why won't you tell me?
You are the begotten.
Tell me,
why don't you
know this by now?

How Love Grows

Often I wish my enemies and
those who try to hurt me an

equal harm, *like to like*—as
anger meets anger and hate

meets hate—but You keep
reminding me, early and late,

that love is *unlike meeting like.*

How You Love

Love is patient, writes the
Apostle, but this is often

what I am *not*, so remind
me to magnify the love

I receive in the waiting,
whether or not this makes

sense, for this is how
You love, and this is

how I am saved.

Love within Reach

Teach me to treasure the
measure of love that mends

the wound that burns night
and day, so that I may learn

that all who wish me ill are
a gift for me, and recall

that all the love in this life
is within reach only when

I let go of the circle of ill
and make room for the love

You ever want to instill.

The Heart's Vision

—An ode to St. Thomas

No one says it like you do,
Thomas—
    the kingdom of God forever.
Not that. No.
It is the simple
    understanding,
the eternal vision of
    affected hearts
known to the Holy One of
    infinite time and space
who speaks and worlds
    are made,
not like kingdoms of earth
    buildings and gold
but love that sees all and
    everywhere, that
    lasts now, as ever,
    as was,
    and is.

Coda of the Heart

—*An ode to Micah 4:5*

The prophet
says
what
God knows.
We will
one day
walk in
the word
of our
Lord,
our God,
not only
forever,
but beyond.

Part Three

THE INNER SPARK

This Inner Spark

There is something
in me so bright and
shining in itself
that the darkness
I fall into or make
whether in despair
or delight cannot
thwart the flow
of this inner light.

Gazing

How can you act like God?
What a thing to even suggest!
I will tell you.
Gaze like the angels do
upon the riches of creation,
including you.

Stop Looking

Uncreated and superlative;
full and complete, without need;
without belonging or belongings;
we who exist can't even testify
    to this
    existence.
Stop your looking.
Know what existence says of Itself,
"I am who I am."

You're So Similar

What could be closer to you than
the One who gave you everything;
who molded you inside,
who stamped you with the divine image,
who made you good, very good?
Nothing is so similar
to something else
as you are to God.

A Still Desert

There is a spark within us
that knows God—an inner

light beyond every kind
of knowing and feeling.

This is a spark that
is one with God, and

when we let ourselves
be alive to this light we

come into a still desert
where all is one
    is God

        is me.

The Kingdom of God, I

> The soul that knows itself
> only in God
> discovers that
> she truly
> is the
> Kingdom of God.

The Kingdom of God, II

—*John 15:21*

So perfection is
already in you.
What does it
matter then that
*they will do all things
to you?*

The Kingdom of God, III

> But listen, Eckhart!
> If you reduce other people,
> you aren't acting from
> that place,
> the Kingdom.
> Is it even yours?

For the Wine

The sweetest wine tastes bitter
when drunk by one who
is ill.
The tongue lies
before the heart
has a chance.

All Those Philosophers

Did you hear the one
about the twenty-four philosophers
who came together to argue
about who God is,
and where God might be found?
They left as they arrived,
confused and blind.

Folding

Let your soul,
your heart,
be folded into the
Holy One
so that nothing at all
will keep the world's
sweetness from you.

What about Church?

You may ask,
"Is church the best place
for me to find God?"
And I will tell you—you are either
in the right state of mind,
possessing God,
or you aren't.
And if you aren't,
God help you,
but not necessarily church.

Pregnant with God

> You are either
> with or
> without.
> I tell you:
> there
> is
> no other.

Three Things Keeping You from Home

There are only three things that keep me
away from my true home.
Hear this, Eckhart!
Don't fuss over that body of yours.
Will the one thing that matters.
And cease your loving of what fades away.
Then and only then
will you see and know the spirit, peace,
and oneness of God.

Still

In my darkness, I often seek You
as if You were a candle to cast light

into the darkness that surrounds me
both by day and through the night,

and when I do, what I find is what
I'd thought I needed, and so I throw

away the candle, and so I turn from
the inner spark with its warming glow

which alone can still my restless heart
and carry my longings back to You.

Within Me in That Soft Place

Within me in the soft place
we call the soul is a fortress

so strong and beyond all
knowing that no one can

enter, not I, not those I
love or fear, not even You.

In this citadel, I am truly
who I am beyond how I

know myself and how
others know me and there

You are truly You beyond
the names we have chosen

to give You, and here we
are not united but one.

You Should Already Know

You should already know
that water flows
downward
into a valley.
But did you know
that the moon
makes it forget
itself, and up
it may stream?

You may want to abandon

> all change, retreating to false
> illusions of your natural state,
> but the source of bliss and joy
> is likely to come when
> you abandon what
> is obvious and natural,
> to go out of
> yourself entirely.

The Deep of My Heart

You join Yourself to me in the simple
ground that is the deep of my heart,

a light untouched by all that was
and is and will be, a gift of water

in the still desert where all is one
in You and You are one with me.

Taking Up a Cross

When Jesus
says, *Take up your
cross and follow
me,*
he means,
Become what
I am, be
right here
in the heart
of God.

Prophets have conquered heaven with faith.

Such an odd thing for
    the God-inspired to say!
But that heaven is common,
    full of places that we know:
the world, which one needs
    a poor spirit to rule.
The body, that one overcomes only
    with hunger and thirst.
And the devil. To conquer it
    we love our pain and grief.

Scaling the Walls

Strange as it sounds,
we scale the walls of
Christ's highest holy place,
never all at once, but
slowly—conversion-style,
finally and only
by love.

Please tell me:

> Why do you do all that fasting?
> Why pray on your knees?
> What's with all the devotions
>   and good works?

> Why be baptized?
> What for?
> Why did God bother with flesh?
> Surely he had other
> things to do.

> Only one reason.

> God wanted to be born in your soul.
> The whole world was born,
> the scriptures bothered to be written,
> to find a home
>   inside you.

Only in My Nakedness

> A many-mansioned house,
> a place of grandeur,
> where no one may buy or sell.
>
> Go your way now.
> There is nothing to buy or sell or see.
>
> My home is in your soul.
> Only I may descend there,
> and only in My nakedness.

If Only I Could

If only
I could.

I do,
I will,
from the heart
easily,
for You.

Obedience
makes
all things
better.

Where Better?

Where better
to find You
than in my
obedience?
If I could only
stop doing
If I could only
stop willing
in my own
furious directions,
there You are.

How Sparks Take Flame

Take note of this, Eckhart!
The more you let go
of what you think
is yours,
is the way toward seeing
how it never was.
And the more you shed
that self and its agenda,
the more you will
see a spark
of God grow,
filling you.

Sparks Don't Ask

Give me this, Lord.
Show me the way.
Reveal to me.
May I share in eternal life.
No, Eckhart!
True obedience makes no requests.
Sparks don't ask
what flames them.
Wanting—douses them for sure.

The Only Prayer with Power

To pray
as God
would have us
do
requires our
minds to be
free.
And freedom
of mind is
achieved only
when we
are unbound
by
devotion,
unattached
to spirituality,
immersed
only
in God.

Stop Your Doing

There is
nothing you
can do,
Eckhart,
to improve on
what is
already
inside you.
Pray with
intensity
with your
whole body,
and don't stop
until you feel
and know
that you
are united
with the One
who animates
those eyes,
ears,
and heart!

Part Four

RADIANCE

Shining Forth

In times of doubt I forget
that You are not a God

of thoughts, to be found
in concepts or theories

but are the source of
my life and the radiance

that shines forth in all
that is, and then I remember:

mine is the work of learning
to see You as the radiance

that shines forth in all that is,
even in the dark. Even in me.

There Is an Antechamber

That temple in
which we usually
find our Lord
is where we
see him shining,
holy.
The intellect goes there.
But when we grasp him—
with fingers and hands?
(of course not)—
in the holy soul, our
birthright, then we really
meet him in the
antechamber.

Acceptance

> If God only is asked
> If only God is desired
> If God answers
> If God sends God
> If we are contented
> If our will is God's will.

When you go outside,

be careful not to lose sight of
the One to whom you
inwardly turn.
That feeling you have
in your cell
or in church,
take it with you. It will
protect you from the rest-
less-

ness.

Nothing can divide you

from the way that you
and God are
together.
You must remember:
You are one
in the One
in whom
there is
only one.

Holy Spirit

When you feel that sweetness,
that immeasurable sweetness,
a rich abundance surrounding you,
even and especially if you have nothing at all,
don't look around: it is your heart that is full.
It is your soul flowing into and out of itself,
through grace with force, and
then, only then, will you be who you are inside.
Jesus has come with the power
of the Holy Spirit. Amen.

Beyond All Names

We speak of You in many names,
You who are beyond all naming.

So take our words and bathe them
in Your radiant silence, so that

we might learn to praise You
beyond our words in every way

we can and in all that is.

Like the Heart

Let me seek You
in the darkness
of my silence

and find You
in the silence
of Your light

which is
love shining
like the sun

flowing
like the river
and joying

like the heart.

How Can I Possess You?

Do not be content with the God
you think about, for when this

thinking comes to an end you lose
the one you thought about as God.

Trust that you already have God
in your heart, for God is always

already there, and in that trust
you will find God shining out

to you in everything in your life.

You Shine in Everything

> Even in the dark of this life
> and in my dark, even there,
> even here, You are radiant
> and meet me there to in-form
> me in Your loving light.

Radiant Darkness

—Psalm 18

Cloud and darkness covered the mountain,
Torah says,
when Moses was upon it.
Sometimes light conceals
more than it reveals
and it is darkness
that's divine.
You may need, like the psalmist,
to make darkness
your covering,
your heaven,
your secret place.

The Source

Just as the sun illumines the air and shines through it,
but keeps its source for itself, so You pour all pleasure

and every delight into every one of your creatures—
and into me—and yet You keep the root of pleasure

and guard delight's essence in Yourself so that
I might seek You as the ever-giving source of

what gives true pleasure and lasting delight.

In the Radiance of Love

In our fear and shame, we see
only a long and lonely darkness.

In your love, You see even this
as a place waiting to be born

in the radiance of love.

Your Only Delight

> There is in me a radiance
> that never ceases, and if
>
> I had eyes to see into the
> darkest depths of my heart
>
> I would know that this inner
> spark is all You ever see
>
> of me, whether by day
> or by night, and this
>
> alone is my one and
> Your only delight.

True Prayer

What is the prayer
of a heart loosed

from all the things
that crowd our lives

and worry our minds
from day to day?

It is coming to that
place within us where

not knowing is the
mark of faith,

not wanting
the work of hope,

and not demanding
the gift of love.

When You Have Lost Something

Consider this, you who have lost something
dear: another might have recovered
something they believed was
forever gone.
Find consolation in this: who wouldn't go
without sight in one eye if it meant
that another could see
forever?

Be on the lookout.

> If you don't truly have God
> within you,
> you will know—
> you'll always
> be looking
> for him somewhere
> else.

You will know

> when God has taken up residence in your heart.
> How?
> Your spirit will move with swiftness and striving;
> you won't be caught just thinking about things.
> For this God of ours is not a God of thoughts
> so much as a God alive.

We All Know, Don't We

We all know, don't we, what St. Jerome
and other greats took for granted:
that each of us has from the start an
angel, or good spirit, and a devil,
inside? Virtue and heaven are
the angel's work, to incessantly
urge and prod, but wickedness and
waste are always the devil's domain.

An evil spirit, that devil, harps
and carps, sweet-talks and dialogues with
us, whispering true sweet-nothings to
the inner ear of every Adam
and every Eve leaning on a tree
flirting with a serpent's vain notions.
Be careful. There is another tree
you can't know but with the Noble Man.

Like a Fire

When I seek what I want
I find this little something
but know nothing of
    Your deep,
and You, my God,
see my ways and turn
from these to keep
    your distance,
for what You want
is my soul stripped of
everything, even true
    desire,
and You burn not
like a candle flickering
in the dark but like a
    fire
flaming the soul when
it seeks nothing but You
and finds everything
    in You.

You Are Not an Answer

> There is no Why in You,
> and so I must learn to trust
>
> that You are not an answer
> to my questions but rather
>
> the source that is true before
> every question I ever had
>
> and the love beyond every
> answer I will ever know.

Beyond Thinking

It is better that I not imagine
that I have You only if I think

the right thoughts about You,
because then I would lose You

as soon as a lover imagines
love to be something we think

and not, as it is, who we are.

Love shines

even as my thoughts about
You fade, for You are always

present to me beyond what
I think or feel or do, and when

I turn to You and accept You
in this simple way, I have You

in every way and in all things
and You shine out in me as

the love that cannot cease.

In This Blinding

When I think that I should know something,
and something great, in order to know You,

I err, because You who are everything are
nothing that could be known for some

purpose, however large or noble. O, give
me this nothing, so that I might love

You who are everything.

Flame My Life

Teach me the humility of knowing
that nothing I can do can grasp

the love that is Your one and ever
hidden work, and let me in my

darkness come to see this nothing
as the radiance that burns until

it finally blinds me, and so flame
my life with the radiance of love

until I finally see.

You Wait for Me

I think mine
is the work
of finding You,

but You wait
for me in my
joy and strife

to reveal
who You are,
which is love,

and to radiate
what You are,
which is light.

Nameless in My Name

You are the One who is in-yet-beyond
the many, Light burning in darkness

and Darkness shining beyond light,
the Good beyond all that is evil, and

the Nothing radiant in all things,
the nameless One in all we name

and the origin that gathers in the end
and is active in every beginning,

the One in my many, Light in my dark,
Dark in my light, Good in my evil and

Nothing in my all, nameless in my
name and Beginning in my end.

Somewhere It Is That's Overgrown

Somewhere it is that's
overgrown,
a convoluted mess
hiding what was planted
inside of me.

Something it is that's
tangled,
where mangrove and ragweed
obscure what still reaches
for light.

Someone it is that's
only God,
Origen says,
who nourishes and soaks
such struggling seeds.

Some day will be when
they'll poke their head
into sun and wind and
find a place, a glorious
place to be.

What I desire

is to act as I know
to do while guarding
myself from worrying

what others think and
whether this is finally
enough, for only then

will I be free to let You
shine as You long to do
in me, and I in You, and

this is finally enough.

Becoming Me

We are born only once
in this world, twice in

You, and in this we are
like You because You

are born not once but
again and again in all

that was and is and
will be. And when You

are born in me I be-
come who You are—

and You become me.

Nothing but Radiance

You are unending life
and love without beginning,

and this is the light that
You pour into my soul

which spills over to all
that I am and was and

will be—love unending
and life without

beginning, love
that becomes nothing

but radiance within me.

Part Five

WITHOUT WHY

At the Heart of Mystery

How are we born in God?
This is a mystery beyond

all that we can know, but
what we can know is

that God is born in us
whenever we begin

to live without a why.

God in Heaven

When God
turns the eye
of that singular
heart, all he sees
is holiness.
Everything,
bound together,
beautifully whole.
This, my friend,
is heaven.

God Is Not a Cow

If you are one of those
who expect to see God
with your own two eyes
remember,
    God is not a cow.
There is no milk and cheese
for you here.
When you make of God
an object,
wanting something,
anything,
    God is not there.

Don't Prattle about God!

> It would be best if I stopped chattering
> and kept silent about You, because when
>
> I speak I say what I do not know, for I
> cannot say what is true about You
>
> who are beyond understanding—
> but not beyond me.

For the Sake of All

In Your first everlasting
glimpse, before time

and space ever were,
You saw everything

in a single moment,
and in that look

gathered all that
was and is and

is to be—even me,
freeing me

to will as You will
for the sake of

love, and to love
as You love

for the sake of all.

Why Me?

> Have you heard about the king
> who accompanied each soldier,
> new recruit, onto the field
> to surprise him, attacking him,
> testing his mettle for battle?
> That king was once nearly killed
> by a servant who fought back,
> and that servant, the king held
> in highest esteem.

Beginning Again

To start a new work
or begin a new life
ask God only to
send you that one
precious sweet desired
thing that is nothing
but all you desire.

Leave God Alone

The greatest honor we can pay to God is
to leave God alone and so be free of God.

Only then can we be true beyond all our
knowing and desiring, and only then

can we find ourselves and

let God be God.

Without Thought of Loving

I only find You when I let go
of what I expect, and I only seek

You truly when I bring my
nothingness to You, beyond

all my certainties and doubts,
for in the hollow of my not-

knowing there is room for the
fullness of Your all-loving,

for You give all of Yourself
without thought of loving,

as simply and wholly as
the sun when it shines

as it ever does.

There Is a Path

There is a path
that God has
given you.
Consider that
you needn't
leave it behind for
another one when other
good things present
themselves.
Bring them along.

Those Who Say

How stupid when
someone says, *She*
suffers because of sin.
My Lord makes clear
that those who
suffer for the sake
of righteousness are
blessed. Blessed.
She is in God's
own hand.

Once the Nobleman Returned

> Once the nobleman returned
> from that far, distant
> land, at once
> strange to him, at
> once too-familiar, ahhh,
> he lost all taste
> for the life he knew.
> All he wanted was to go back
> once again
> to that distant country.
> He'd become a ruler of a kingdom
> of nothing,
> but everything.

If I hope to know You

I must seek an unknowing
that is not a lack but

my only gain, taking me
beyond the press

of demands and desires
to an emptiness

where there is room for
You to be born

beyond all that I demand
to know and desire

to find, for You birth
the Word in

my silence and burn
as light in

my darkness.

The All of Ever Only Love

> We name the world
>> of things and feelings, of this and
>> of that, of yes and of no, of dark
>> and of light,
> and in all this
>> turn from the source of our being
>> which has no name we can know
>> and is beyond
> every feeling
>> and cannot be other than yes,
>> and when I give myself to
>> the inflow of
> me into You
>> I find that this origin is the way
>> and this way is the end and
>> this end is the all of
> ever only love.

Here and Now

Everything hangs on the little word
here and its sibling *now*, but I often

forget this, keeping busy with my
plans, building for a future I cannot

know and against worries I cannot
finally tame, and yet You wait

for me to come home to Your *now*
which is beyond past and future,

and return to Your *here* which is
present before beginning and

beyond every ending.

Give Me Words That Sing

Teach me, I pray, to see the small
unnoticed things in my life,

close to my reach and deeper
than my eye alone can teach.

Show me with the steady measure
of a poet's gaze what it means

to seek words that are pleasing
and alive, as the dance is

to those with tired legs and knees.
Give me words that sing

against the darkest nowhere hour,
ones full of enough silence to be

rich in the spin of every *now* and
alive in the tremble of each *here*.

The Yes of Your Word

Let me learn to weave of the threads of my life
a fabric soft and warm and colorful enough

to wrap me with love as I long to be, and let me
find the courage to know that who I am

gives life to the always *now* and ever *here* of love,
and let me believe that it is enough to let the *Yes*

of Your Word rise to bursting life in me.

Wonder

Now listen:
Death is
not real
unless you
neglect to
leave life
        behind.

Your Soul's Delight

There is a journey
you must take.
It is a journey without destination.
There is no map.
Your soul will lead you.
And you can take nothing with you.

The One Nameless Truth

You, nameless God, want to form
Yourself in me and give Yourself

to me, not as I think or want or will
but rather as You are, beyond all

thinking and wanting and willing
in the one nameless truth of love.

Beyond, I

In you is no less or more to see or
sense, no this or that, no here
or there, no then or now,

because You are ever yes
and always in all and
beyond every thing
that is or will be.

Beyond, II

You are beyond seeing and naming and knowing
and loving and You remain the no-thing who Is

and the no-being who is not beyond and remains
in what was and is and will be and You are

the light that shines in the dark that is my life and
the Yes that sings in the No of no-thing-ness and

the song of everywhereness in what is and will be.

All or Nothing

Only in the all of the Spirit are
we able to open ourselves to

the one great work, which is to
let go of everything, even love,

so in our emptiness we might
have room enough, possessing

nothing—neither virtue nor vice
nor love itself nor its absence—

and so finding You.

Becoming Emptiness

Our work is simply this: to become
the emptiness that can receive,

like the thirst that brings us
to the well, the dryness

that causes water to run uphill,
and become simple enough

to receive the one who is nothing,
and empty enough to hunger

for the nothing that is God,
which even then is love.

Ever Shining Light

Some days it seems the whole world
is tilting the wrong way: it might be up

but I am somehow down, and right is
always somewhere else against my

wrong, and then You remind me that
within me burns an ever shining light

which no night or stumbling down
can ever fully dim or finally smite.

Your Single Yes of Love

Often little things annoy me
    and the big ones seem to gallop
with their shades of gloom
    and shake off even the radiant

sun-splashed light of today,
    and I know I should hoe the
virtue of patience but do not,
    and all my hurry unravels

my careful plans for calm
    and worries away thoughts
of long-off better times.
    And then I hear You say again

that You are without why
    and ask that I let go of
all this in the simple joy
    of Your single Yes of Love.

The Gift

You are the light that
fire-flames me and I am the dark
that still blames me.

You are the love that
help-holds me and I am the hate
that still scolds me.

You are the song that
pure-molds me, reminding me of love
that enfolds me.

You are the gift that
new-names me and shines as a light
that enflames me.

I Need Not Speak

The Lord touched my mouth
and spoke.

Without sound my Lord
filled me.

I had chattered, my
heart spun,

Words flying, birds in-
to air.

But that touch to my
mouth stopped

God's going out, and
now my

Lord—I can hear you
inside.

Prayers Like Stones

A monk rose from his knees and
declared the grandeur of God:

All praise and glory are Yours,
Father, Son, and Holy Spirit.

Be quiet, hushed his brother
in the dark, from the next cell,

you dishonor the One
you most intend to praise.

Listen to this stone; it too
is an utterance of God.

Dizzy

The holy word
that first made,
then acted as
living speech,
has kissed my mouth,
choosing me.
Now I'm dizzy.

Making Room

Just as a single barrel cannot hold
two different drinks at once, so too
the heart must empty itself of water
if we wish to fill our lives with wine.

Your First Work

> You flow into all that is, creatures
> and things, high and low, things
>
> in the heavens and things here
> below, and do this not because
>
> You have any need of them or
> of me, but because You cannot
>
> do other and in this inflowing
> give to each and every creature
>
> and to me the capacity to work,
> and Your first work is the heart.

Sometimes I feel

like giving up. It's just too
much work, this being me—

too much pain, this be-me-ing,
too much dark, this me-ing-be,

and then You remind me
that my nothing is Your all,

and Your all my truest
deepest call.

From Being-Me to Being-We

When I lose myself in fear
and its other side, blame,

You tell me to take my
being-me and give it

to your being-You,
which is ever full of

unbecoming is-ness
and unnameable no-

thing-ness, so that
together we might

become a single
and simple being-we.

Gravity Is the Way

Gravity is the way You
dwell in this world

and in me, the way
Love comes down

to us and will not
let us go, ever,

no matter what.

Seeking the Dark

In the downward
spiral of love

You can do nothing
other than fall

and so come close
to us, becoming

who You are,
like a stone

thrown in a wide
arc into a deep

canyon, seeking the
dark where

all that is comes
alive in all

You are.

The Gravity of Love

You are the one
who falls so that

You can find me in
the deep and down-

ward tumble of life,
like a stone that

descends in tend-
ing ever down

to where it comes
to rest, and just so,

there where I fall
is where You

wait and how
You call.

Upward Gravity

O fall with me all the long
way down, and so reach

me through the call that
rises impossibly as

the upward gravity
of love.

On Our Best Days

On our best days and our worst, in times both
clever and confused, our life is finally summed

in this: we are made to love without reason,
to breathe in the wide open plain of wonder,

to ponder without asking why,

because in God there is no why
to be found, no reason to be known

beyond the flame of ever whyless love.

Giver and Gift

All that I have and all I ever
will is on temporary loan,

given for a season like the leaves
of spring that soon enough will

rustle in the late autumn winds,
for You give with a single intent:

that I might know that You are
Giver and Gift, the one beyond

any how and every why, one
I didn't earn and can never lose,

and one that will never lose me.

In this present moment

>I am free,
>or, I am trying to be
>free and empty
>of all that
>I have done and seen.

If I could be free

> I would be without child,
> so to speak, bearing no fruit,
> causing no stir.
> I would be the only spouse
> to my only One.

The Fruit of God in Me

There is noble ground and
my only One has tilled it.
His seed flowers, and colors,
ripe with sweet savor,
and I hardly know now
the taste of this virginal me.

All Will Be Well

My work is to be empty enough
to make room for You to fill me

entirely with love, and when You
do I find that I have room for all

that is because You become love
in what I am and think and do,

and my heart becomes so full
of You that love is my all and

all will be well with me.

If

If I could love
    as God loves
I would not
    fear the judgment
of others
    or the loss of my
very self and would
    know that God is
the one who knows
    and loves and desires
himself and all
    things and loves
me most when
    I finally let go of
trying and simply
    let myself live love.

To Let Go of All

The cup must be empty
to find its true meaning

beyond every kind of
usefulness, so empty

that it would not know
why it is a cup or to

what end, poor and use-
less and without a single

purpose it could know,
which is what I, too,

must learn to be if I
would be free, striving

to let go of all I hope
might fill me so that all

that is finally left is God.

Finally

I sometimes think of my flaws
as a burden that keeps me a

stranger to myself and others,
and then suddenly remember

that God made me this way

so that through my flaws I might
learn to crave love even more

and let God be finally God.

My God Is

My God is
love absolutely,
purely and simply,
in all, through all, and from all.
My God is
the one who is desired
by everyone who desires
and loves.

Big and Sweet

There is a love that fills the universe so completely and richly that it is impossible to separate from itself. It is a holiness, a blessed everlastingness, that is indivisible and so sweet. You will never see or comprehend it, or pin it down, but it gives of itself without thinking, like the warm light of the sun in the morning.

Don't Thank God

Don't thank God
for loving you.
God could do no other.

Don't thank God
for a soul that's noble.
It simply is.

Thank God for
this pulsing divine life
and pray God to throb it.

Then

If I could
trust that
You are enough
I would know
that I am
enough.

All That Baggage, I

> Where the creaturely
> ends in me is where
>
> God has the room
> to begin, on the far
>
> side of my desires
> and demands, beyond
>
> my expectations and
> worries and needs.

All That Baggage, II

When I let go of all that,
like letting a heavy sack

drop from my drooping
shoulders, God has room

to be God within me,
and I wonder what

I thought I needed
with all that baggage

in the first place.

What I want

is
everything.
And God, too.
What I have
is
the sense
of desiring,
without everything,
and not even
a trace of
God.
What if
next time
I sought God
and left
everything
else alone?

God beyond Seeking

When I seek God
with something in mind,

the best I get is
the something I had

in mind.

Enough Now

Enough with words, now.
This is more than enough.
Shhhhh
Enough. Go.

An Afterword:
Seeking God on the Wayless Way

Meister Eckhart once wrote that those seeking God who do so in "a certain way" end up with that "way" but fail to find God. Ours is the task, he went on to say, of learning to seek God "without a way" and "without a why," meaning to open ourselves to the surprising and often unsettling adventure that constitutes this search. He also knew that the search for God was a search for the self, and that this was a search not without purpose but surely without end. "Of God you can never have a sufficiency, since the more you have him the more you desire him," he said, concluding, "If you could ever have enough of God so that you were contented with him, then God would not be God." This is how we come to know that there is no "end" nor is there a "why" in God.

Eckhart has always stood out in the history of Christian mystics as unique. He blended Platonic thought with Christian theology. He lived and wrote attending to the great theological paradox that the God who is no/thing is in all things, and beyond all things—including our ways of thinking and speaking about God. He could even speak of God not simply as a "beingness" beyond nothing, as one might expect of a Platonist, but more daringly as "a nothingness beyond being." What this could possibly mean, he insists, awaits our discovering in the thick texture of our lives and not in the thin stuff of thought, however elaborate and serious this might be.

Language was both the great obstacle and the great vehicle of this adventure, for Eckhart; it was both the problem and solution to our longing for the divine. To discover this, he once suggested, what we most need is "emphatic speech." But our desires usually lead us in indirect and circuitous routes to such language. Thus, his is an example of the wandering mind that seeks what it cannot know and comes to know that its longings bring us to an ongoing life of seeking.

The appeal of Eckhart has always been strongest among those who try to live contemplatively in the world. Thomas Merton, Trappist monk and writer, once noted in his private journal that "I am becoming entranced with Eckhart: I have been won by the brevity, the incisiveness of his sermons, his way of piercing straight to the heart of the inner life, the awakened spark, the creative and redeeming word, God born in us."[1] Above all, Eckhart knew that we are most alive in the

---

[1] Thomas Merton, *Turning Toward the World: The Pivotal Years. Journals, Vol. 4: 1960–1963*, ed. Victor A. Kramer (San Francisco: HarperCollins, 1996), 137.

vital contradiction that our work is not to "find ourselves," as we are wont to put it these days, but to "lose" ourselves, by which he means letting go of the "self" we think we are and opening ourselves to what lies beyond the narrower confines of our knowing. "Examine yourself, and wherever you find yourself, take leave of yourself. This is the best way of all," he once wrote. Or again: "You must know that there is no one in this life who has let go of himself so much that he did not find that he could let go even more."

Whatever we think of him, Eckhart was most of all a puzzle. Some branded him a heretic in his own day; some still do. For others, he stands as a signal light of vital spiritual engagement, a voice from the Middle Ages whose distance in time has lost nothing of its urgency and profundity. Perhaps his voice has an even stronger eloquence now than it did in his own times.

What we love about Eckhart is that he both embodied and then contradicted the psalmist who prayed: "O Lord . . . I do not occupy myself with things too great and too marvelous for me. But I have calmed and quieted my soul, like a weaned child with its mother." (Psalms 131:1–2) Our basic nature is to reach for things that are beyond our grasp. This includes our spiritual longings, which are not satisfied with what we can know.

For the mystic Eckhart, the world is true, not statements about it, and God is true, never to be captured or pinpricked in our conceptions and not to be limited by our strongest hopes or fears.

But—and this, too, is what we love about him—although he wants to be quiet in the face of a silent God, he just can't. It is this blend of reluctance and exuberance which makes him a voice so suited to the ponderings of modern women and men. For Eckhart knew that the settled conventions of religion often find little resonance in the aching and longing places within us that we have come to think of as our "heart." Beyond religion, beyond faith, we come to know what it means to be on "the wayless way." And only so do we begin to realize the Meister's startling claim that "the eye with which I see God is exactly the same eye with which God sees me. My eye and God's eye are one eye, one seeing, one knowledge, and one love." This is the finding we do not know to seek and the seeking that finds us for who we truly are—one seeing, one knowledge, and one love.

Notes and Sources for the Poems

Sources

In the notes to the poems, references to various collections of Eckhart's sermons and writings are indicated below.

Deutsche Predigten: Meister Eckehart. Deutsche Predigten und Traktate. Edited and translated into modern German by Josef Quint. München: Carl Hanser Verlag, 1979.

Einheit im Sein: Meister Eckhart. Einheit im Sein und Wirken. Translated, edited, and introduced by Dietmar Mieth. Munich and Zurich: R. Piper, 1986.

Essential Sermons: Meister Eckhart. The Essential Sermons, Commentaries, Treatises, and Defense. Translated into English and Introduced by Edmund Colledge, OSA, and Bernard McGinn. New York: Paulist Press, 1981.

....

Selected Writings: Meister Eckhart. Selected Writings. Selected and translated into English by Oliver Davies. New York: Penguin, 1994.

Teacher and Preacher: Meister Eckhart. Teacher and Preacher. Edited and translated into English by Bernard McGinn, with the Collaboration of Frank Tobin and Elvira Borgstadt. New York: Paulist Press, 1986.

....

Notes

[in the order in which they appear]

Opening the Heart's Door. See *Selected Writings* 226–28.

PART ONE. OUR SOUL-LIFE

Look Quietly. From "Talks of Instruction," 7; see
Selected Writings 13.

Sometimes You Have to Break Things. See *Selected Writings* 11.

What Do You See? From "Book of Divine Consolation"; see
Selected Writings 64.

Nine Words of Prayer. From Latin sermon 4, see
Selected Writings 264–65.

Can You Do This? See *Selected Writings* 244–45.

Can You See? From German sermon 29; see *Selected Writings*
239–40.

What I Want Is Joy. See *Essential Sermons* 294.

Your Silence. From "Talks of Instruction"; see *Selected Writings* 43.

....

Room to Grow. See *Essential Sermons* 292–93.

All and Ever Only Love. See *Selected Writings* 210.

Obedience. See *Einheit im Sein* 168.

Breaking Through. See *Selected Writings* 11.

A Soul Digests. See *Teacher and Preacher* 257–58.

The Way Love Is. See *Teacher and Preacher* 215.

A Single Undivided Love. See *Deutsche Predigten* 292.

In Each Moment. See *Teacher and Preacher* 240–43.

The One. See *Selected Writings*, 163–64.

Consider the Moon. See *Teacher and Preacher* 259, with a veiled quoting of Sirach 50:6.

Gratitude. See *Teacher and Preacher* 213.

In All That Is. See *Selected Writings* 10–11.

Study the Stone. See *Selected Writings* 76.

You Taste Us. See *Deutsche Predigten* 272.

Becoming Love, I. See *Teacher and Preacher* 240.

The Descent of Love. See *Teacher and Preacher* 251.

Emptiness. See *Selected Writings* 227–29.

Outside of Space and Time. See *Selected Writings* 263.

Love's Delights. See *Teacher and Preacher* 272.

If I Hope to Know You. See *Selected Writings* 220–22.

An Unknowing That Makes Room. See *Selected Writings* 217–19.

Joy Meets Joy. See *Selected Writings* 217–19.

You Rise by Stooping Down. See *Teacher and Preacher* 273.

A Human Heart Pounds. This string poem comes from a sermon preached on the text of Matthew. 22:42; the closing lines of the poem then also refer to Deuteronomy. 6:5. See *Selected Writings* 263–64.

How We Fit. See *Selected Writings* 230–31.

Nothing of My Deeds. See *Teacher and Preacher* 296.

God's Unending Now. See *Selected Writings* 123.

Risking Unknowing. See *Selected Writings* 219–21.

More God. See *Selected Writings* 236–37.

PART TWO. LETTING GO

The Rest. See *Selected Writings* 231.

Our Secret Entry. See *Essential Sermons* 292.

Alternatives. From "Talks of Instruction"; see
   Selected Writings 43.

The Man with Money. From "Book of Divine Consolation"; see
   Selected Writings 60.

This Is What You Desired. From "Book of Divine Consolation";
   see *Selected Writings* 63.

Don't Work So Hard. See *Selected Writings* 138.

Lose Yourself! See *Essential Sermons* 248–49.

Becoming Love, II. See *Essential Sermons* 253.

Where I Stop, You Begin. See *Essential Sermons* 184.

Letting Go. See *Selected Writings* 222–25.

Enough. See *Essential Sermons* 276–77.

Truth Does Not Like Business Deals. See *Teacher and Preacher* 240. The title of the poem is a direct quote from Eckhart.

What Then of You? See *Selected Writings* 178.

Making Space. See *Essential Sermons* 291.

Become Empty. See *Selected Writings* 227.

We Must Abandon God. See *Selected Writings* 177.

Only My Nothingness. See *Deutsche Predigten* 53–54.

Desiring Nothing and Seeking Nothing. See *Selected Writings* 140.

A Single Mind. See *Deutsche Predigten* 54.

....

Even More. This is one of the root motifs of Eckhart's thought, an experience of loosing our hold of things that he often calls "Gelassenheit," a word he coined that is difficult to describe in English. It literally means a "letting-be-ness," an experience sometimes rendered—as in the standard English translations of Heidegger—as "releasement." See *Deutsche Predigten* 57.

Forgetting to Remember. See *Deutsche Predigten* 290–92.

Paradox. See *Selected Writings* 237.

Only when I let go. See *Deutsche Predigten* 290–92.

Love Is the Lure. See *Selected Writings* 229.

Moses. From Eckhart's "Commentary on Exodus"; see *Teacher and Preacher* 45.

Behind You. See *Teacher and Preacher* 268.

Sweet Darkness. From the "Commentary on Exodus"; see *Teacher and Preacher* 45.

Jesus in the Temple. See *Teacher and Preacher* 239.

Good People. See *Teacher and Preacher* 240.

Every Angel. See *Teacher and Preacher* 269.

What then should I do. See *Selected Writings* 236.

Unlearning, Lesson I; Lesson II; and Lesson III. Selections from the "Commentary on the Book of Wisdom"; see *Teacher and Preacher* 147–50.

How Love Grows. See *Essential Sermons* 150.

How You Love. See *Essential Sermons* 150.

Love within Reach. See *Essential Sermons* 150.

The Heart's Vision; and, Coda of the Heart. From the "Commentary on Exodus"; see *Teacher and Preacher* 73.

PART THREE. THE INNER SPARK

This Inner Spark. See *Selected Writings* 135–46.

Gazing. German sermon 29; see *Selected Writings* 240.

Stop Looking. From the "Commentary on Exodus"; see *Teacher and Preacher* 68.

You're So Similar. From the "Commentary on Exodus"; see *Teacher and Preacher* 82.

A Still Desert. See *Selected Writings* 136.

The Kingdom of God, I. See *Selected Writings* 248–49.

The Kingdom of God, II; and, The Kingdom of God, III. See *Selected Writings* 250.

For the Wine. From "The Book of Divine Consolation"; see *Selected Writings* 87–88.

All Those Philosophers. See *Teacher and Preacher* 255–56.

Folding. From "The Book of Divine Consolation"; see *Selected Writings* 87–88.

What about Church? and, Pregnant with God. See *Selected Writings* 9.

Three Things Keeping You from Home. See *Teacher and Preacher* 267.

Still. See *Teacher and Preacher* 250.

Within Me in That Soft Place. This text voices Eckhart's response to what it means that the soul is like when, as he puts it in the German sermon on Luke 10:38, "Our Lord Jesus Christ entered a citadel and was received by a virgin who was a wife." This citadel, he suggests, is the soul, and no one, not even God, can enter that citadel without giving up everything that seems necessary to "be" God: namely, the divine nature, the persons of the Trinity itself, the names by which God comes to be known, etc. See *Selected Writings*, 158–59.

You Should Already Know; and, You may want to abandon. From "The Book of Divine Consolation"; see *Selected Writings* 82.

The Deep of My Heart. See *Selected Writings* 135–36.

Taking Up a Cross. From "The Book of Divine Consolation"; see *Selected Writings* 82–83.

Prophets have conquered heaven with faith; and, Scaling the Walls. See *Selected Writings* 111.

Please tell me. See *Selected Writings* 112–18.

Only in My Nakedness. The opening four lines of this poem are biblical ideas, taken from John 14:2, Baruch 3:24, and Matthew 21:12, the second and third of which are quoted by Eckhart in a sermon; see *Selected Writings* 255–57.

If Only I Could; and, Where Better? From "Talks of Instruction"; see *Selected Writings* 3.

How Sparks Take Flame; and, Sparks Don't Ask. From "Talks of Instruction"; see *Selected Writings* 4.

The Only Prayer with Power. From "Talks of Instruction"; see *Selected Writings* 4–5.

Stop Your Doing. From "Talks of Instruction"; see *Selected Writings* 5.

PART FOUR. RADIANCE

Shining Forth. See *Selected Writings* 10.

There Is an Antechamber. See *Teacher and Preacher* 257.

Acceptance. From "Talks of Instruction"; see *Selected Writings* 43.

When you go outside; and, Nothing can divide you. See *Selected Writings* 9.

Holy Spirit. German sermon 1; see *Teacher and Preacher* 243.

Beyond All Names. See *Teacher and Preacher* 128–29.

Like the Heart. See *Teacher and Preacher* 212–14.

How Can I Possess You? See *Selected Writings* 10.

You Shine in Everything. From "The Talks of Instruction"; see *Selected Writings* 10–11.

Radiant Darkness. From "Commentary on Exodus"; see *Teacher and Preacher* 117.

The Source. See *Selected Writings* 142.

In the Radiance of Love. See *Teacher and Preacher* 152–53.

Your Only Delight. See *Selected Writings* 135–36.

True Prayer. See *Essential Sermons* 292.

When You Have Lost Something. From "Book of Divine Consolation"; see *Selected Writings* 67–68.

Be on the lookout; and, You will know. See *Selected Writings* 10.

We All Know, Don't We. This two-stanza poem follows a simple pattern of nine syllables per line. It only slightly rephrases the fourth paragraph from "On the Noble Man." For Eckhart, these angels and demons are not exterior to the human soul, but within it—almost like Goethe in *Faust* I: "*Zwei Seelen wohnen, ach! In meiner Brust.*" ("Oh, two souls live in my breast!"). See *Selected Writings* 99–100.

Like a Fire. See *Teacher and Preacher* 250.

You Are Not an Answer. See *Selected Writings* 240.

Beyond Thinking. See *Essential Sermons* 253.

Love shines. See *Essential Sermons* 253.

In This Blinding. See *Teacher and Preacher* 323–25.

Flame My Life. See *Teacher and Preacher* 323–25.

You Wait for Me. See *Teacher and Preacher* 267.

Nameless in My Name. See *Teacher and Preacher* 320.

Somewhere It Is That's Overgrown. From "On the Noble Man"; see *Selected Writings* 100–102.

What I desire. See *Essential Sermons* 274–75.

Becoming Me. See *Selected Writings* 216.

Nothing but Radiance. See *Selected Writings* 216.

PART FIVE. WITHOUT WHY

At the Heart of Mystery. See *Selected Writings* 142.

God in Heaven. See *Selected Writings* 239.

God Is Not a Cow. See *Teacher and Preacher* 278.

Don't Prattle about God! See *Selected Writings* 236.

For the Sake of All. See *Essential Sermons* 289–93.

Why Me? From "The Book of Divine Consolation"; see *Selected Writings* 84.

Beginning Again. From "Talks of Instruction"; see *Selected Writings* 42.

Leave God Alone. See *Selected Writings* 244–45.

Without Thought of Loving. See *Teacher and Preacher* 212–15.

There Is a Path. From "Talks of Instruction"; see
 Selected Writings 43.

Those Who Say. From "The Book of Divine Consolation"; see
 Selected Writings 90.

Once the Nobleman Returned. This poem is a summary of the
 first three paragraphs of Eckhart's short treatise, "On the
 Noble Man." See *Selected Writings* 99.

If I hope to know You. See *Selected Writings* 220–22.

The All of Ever Only Love. See *Teacher and Preacher* 322.

Here and Now. This poem takes its inspiration from "The Talks
 of Instruction," especially chapter 6: "Whoever truly pos-
 sesses God in the right way, possesses God in all places: on
 the street, in any company, as well as in a church or a remote
 place or [where they dwell]." See *Selected Writings* 8–12.

Give Me Words That Sing. From "The Talks of Instruction";
 Teacher and Preacher 12–13.

The Yes of Your Word. From "The Book of Divine Consolation"; see *Selected Writings* 60–91.

Wonder. See *Selected Writings* 246.

Your Soul's Delight. See *Selected Writings* 246–47.

The One Nameless Truth. See *Teacher and Preacher* 322.

Beyond, I and Beyond, II. These "string" poems touch on a central theme found throughout Eckhart's writings: viz., the mysterious truth that there is an inviolable unity within each human being, which he sometimes calls a "citadel," that nothing—not our foolishness or wickedness, not our sin or our confusion—can erase. Our work is to come to realize this essential oneness. The poem that follows points to the stunning consequence Eckhart draws from this. See *Selected Writings*, 163–64.

All or Nothing; and, Becoming Emptiness. These themes are found in many of Eckhart's sermons, featuring centrally in "The Book of Divine Consolation." Here, the Meister suggests that, in emptying ourselves of everything—our fears, our expectations, our hopes, and our faith itself—we become capable of receiving God. "Emptiness draws water uphill and causes many other miracles of which we cannot speak here," he writes in the second chapter of this book. See *Selected Writings* 69.

Ever Shining Light. This poem finds its inspiration in "The Book of Consolation" where the Meister writes: "There is an inner work which neither time nor space can support or contain and in which there is something which is divine and akin to God and which, similarly, is beyond time and space. . . . Also we cannot impede the inner activity of virtue any more than we can God. This activity shines out day and night." See *Selected Writings* 75.

Your Single Yes of Love. From "The Book of Divine Consolation"; see *Selected Writings* 70–81.

The Gift. See *Teacher and Preacher* 320–25.

I Need Not Speak. See *Selected Writings* 127–30.

Prayers Like Stones. See *Selected Writings* 127–30.

Dizzy. See *Selected Writings* 127–30.

Making Room. This poem finds its origin in "The Book of Divine Consolation" where Eckhart writes: "No barrel can hold two different drinks. If it is to contain wine, then the water must be poured out so that the barrel is quite empty. Therefore, if you wish to be filled with God and divine joy, then you must pour the creatures out of yourself. St. Augustine says: 'Pour out, so that you may be filled. Turn away, so that you may be turned towards.'" See *Selected Writings* 68–69.

Your First Work. See *Teacher and Preacher* 321.

Sometimes I feel. This poem takes as its point of departure lines from the German sermon on Ephesians 4.23, "You shall be renewed in your spirit." See *Selected Writings* 235–39.

From Being-Me to Being-We. See *Selected Writings* 235–38.

Gravity Is the Way. This poem gives voice to Eckhart's claim that "I say the same of those who have destroyed themselves as they exist in themselves, in God and in all creatures. Such people have taken up the lowest position, and God must pour the whole of himself into them—or he would not be God." See *Selected Writings* 134.

Seeking the Dark. See *Teacher and Preacher* 320.

....

The Gravity of Love. See *Teacher and Preacher* 321.

Upward Gravity. See *Teacher and Preacher* 321.

On Our Best Days. See *Selected Writings* 80–81.

Giver and Gift. See *Essential Sermons* 275.

In this present moment; If I could be free; and, The Fruit of God in Me. These three short poems are interrelated; see *Selected Writings* 158–60.

All Will Be Well. See *Essential Sermons* 254.

If. From "The Book of Divine Consolation"; see *Selected Writings* 64.

To Let Go of All. From "The Book of Divine Consolation"; see *Selected Writings* 70.

Finally. From "The Book of Divine Consolations"; see *Selected Writings* 67.

My God Is. See *Teacher and Preacher* 212–13.

....

Big and Sweet. See *Teacher and Preacher* 213.

Don't Thank God. See *Teacher and Preacher* 213–14.

Then. See *Essential Sermons* 276–77.

All That Baggage, I and II. See *Deutsche Predigten*, 180–81.

What I want. See *Deutsche Predigten* 180.

God beyond Seeking. See *Deutsche Predigten* 180.

Enough Now. From "The Book of Divine Consolation"; see
Selected Writings 91, and elsewhere.

About the Authors

Jon M. Sweeney is an independent scholar and critic, and writer. Among his many works is the popular history, *The Pope Who Quit: A True Medieval Tale of Mystery, Death, and Salvation.*

He is the publisher and editor-in-chief at Paraclete Press and lives in Milwaukee, Wisconsin.

Mark S. Burrows is a poet and scholar of medieval theology. His poems and translations have appeared in *Poetry, The Cortland Review, Southern Quarterly,* and *Weavings,* among others. His recent publications include two volumes of German poetry in translation: Rilke's *Prayers of a Young Poet* and the German-Iranian poet SAID's *99 Psalms.*

He serves as professor of religion and literature at the Protestant University of Applied Sciences in Bochum, Germany.